The Children's Book

WALKER BOOKS
LONDON

Ron van der Meer

Foreword

When Nick Butterworth suggested this book to Save the Children in February 1985, we gave his idea an enthusiastic welcome. There was only one problem – could it possibly be produced in time for Christmas? The answer was yes, thanks to the determination of everyone concerned to help the victims of Africa's devastating famine. I send my warmest gratitude to them all for making this delightful book possible. Nick joined forces with the publishers, Walker Books. Together they contacted the authors, illustrators, designers, reproduction house, typesetters, printers and booksellers. They all donated their services or provided them at cost so that the book could raise the maximum amount of money for Save the Children Fund's famine relief work.

That money – every penny of it – will be desperately needed. Already Save the Children has mounted its biggest ever emergency operation in Sudan and Ethiopia: running feeding and medical centres, airlifting food and supplies, providing trucks and logistics experts to help with distribution. As I write this message we still do not know whether the rains will come this year, but even if they do, we know that the harvest will not be good; the whole agricultural system has been disrupted as people have been forced to leave their homes in search of food. Save the Children's emergency aid will be needed far into 1986, and when at last this drought is over we shall have our part to play in the battle to ensure that future droughts will never again bring such appalling famine in their wake.

Giles Witherington
Chairman
Save the Children

*

The credits that appear after each poem list the author first, then the illustrator. One name appears for contributors who are both the author and illustrator.

MRS CHRISTMAS
(for Tarot Couzyn)

She was about as small as a cup
But big as your head when she grew up
And she came to stay on Christmas Day
So we called her Mrs Christmas

She liked to swoosh around the hall
With a silver paper soccer ball
And I think I was four but maybe some more
When I named her Mrs Christmas

She had some kittens with bright white socks
And she kept them in a brown cardboard box
And she'd nudge them out and march them about
Saying: 'I am Mrs Christmas.'

Adrian Mitchell / Nicola Bayley

Late on a summer's day
When no one else is there,
Tobias comes to smoke his pipe
And take the evening air.

Resting on the soft green moss
He smiles and winks his eye,
Remembering the boggy days
Of summers long gone by.

Peter Weevers

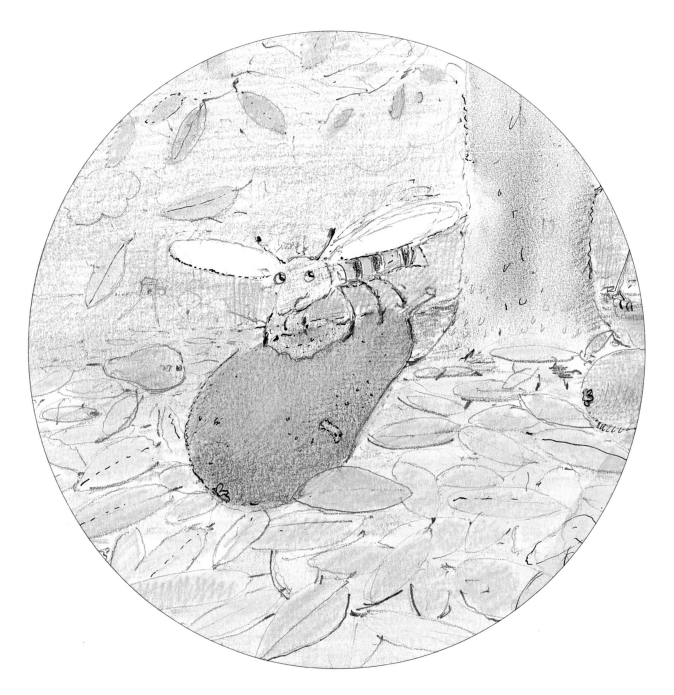

To buzz about the air, or ground
Is fun I do declare,
But ecstasy can best be found,
Inside a rotten pear.

John Burningham

THE WORLD IS FLAT

Where I come from,
Said the man in the hat,
It's a common belief
That the world is flat.
People may mock me,
And people may scoff,
But I know someone
Who's fallen off.

Michael Palin/Michael Foreman

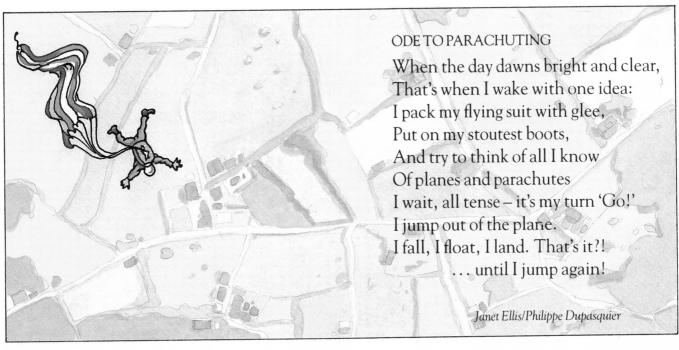

ODE TO PARACHUTING

When the day dawns bright and clear,
That's when I wake with one idea:
I pack my flying suit with glee,
Put on my stoutest boots,
And try to think of all I know
Of planes and parachutes
I wait, all tense – it's my turn 'Go!'
I jump out of the plane.
I fall, I float, I land. That's it?!
    . . . until I jump again!

Janet Ellis/Philippe Dupasquier

THE COWBOY'S SHAME

The name of Frank Carew Macgraw
Was notorious in the West,
Not as the fastest on the draw
But cause he only wore a vest.

Yes just a vest and nothing more!
Through the Wild and Woolly West,
They knew the name of Frank Macgraw
Cause he only wore a vest.

Oh! His nether parts swung wild and free
As on his horse he sat.
He wore a vest and nothing else –
Oh! except a cowboy hat.

Yes! naked from the waist he rode –
He did not give two hoots!
Frank Macgraw in hat and vest
Oh! and a pair of boots.

But nothing else – no! not a stitch!
As through the cactus he
Rode on his horse, although of course
He did protect his knee

With leather leggings – but that's all!
No wonder that his name
Was infamous throughout the West
And spoken of with shame.

Actually he *did* wear pants
On Sunday, and it's true
He also wore them other days –
And sometimes he wore two!

And often in an overcoat
You'd see him riding by,
But as he went men shook their heads
And ladies winked their eye,

For *everyone* knew Frank Macgraw
Throughout the Old Wild West –
Not because he broke the law
But cause he *only* wore a vest!

Terry Jones / Tony Ross

13

CORONATION TREAT!

Young King John at twenty-one
   was crowned, which made him flustered.
He placed his crown on a pudding plate
   and covered it with custard.

His sister, rushing up, declared,
   'The jewels, it'll rot 'em!'
Alas, she tripped and sprawled and slipped
   and landed on her . . . brother!

And as they rolled around the floor,
   hysterical, their pup
Thought, 'Din-dins, great!' and ate
   the custard, gold and jewels right up!

That night a formal ball required
   King John with crown! Instead
He took his dog along with him
   And wore that on his head!

Brian Cant / Chris Winn

There once was a very fat rabbit,
Which had an unrabbit-like habit.
If it smelt toasted cheese,
Just a whiff, on the breeze,
It would jettison lettuce and grab it.

Bamber Gascoigne / Christina Gascoigne

Look at the clock,
  Look at the time.
It's time for school,
  It's five to nine.

Look at the clock,
  Look at the door.
It's time to go home,
  It's ten to four.

Anna Barton / John Vernon Lord

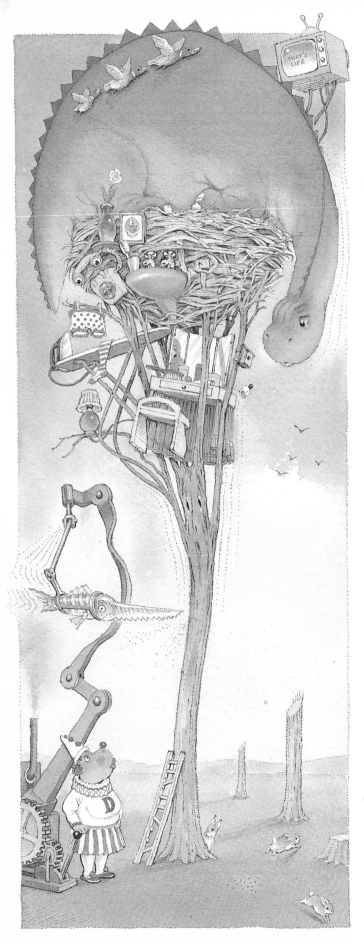

A dinosaur lived in our town
But Dinah his wife was a clown.
He admitted to me
We once lived in a tree
Till the day Dinah sawed the tree down!

Esther Rantzen / Peter Cross

THE MAD HOUSE

We had a dog, her name was Peg
She bit the postman on the leg.
He came around to tell my mum
So Peg then bit him on the bum.

Jane Parrish / Rosalinda Kightley

What do you do, folks ask me
When you've problems of your own?
I talk, I reply, to Benjie, my cat
Who snuggles inside my husband's best hat
And with two men like this
My life is sheer bliss
And I'm never, ever, alone.
       Touch wood...

Marjorie Proops / Jane Johnson

Rover digs the most dreadful holes
when he buries his bones,
And the air is flying with mud and sticks,
worms and stones,
While dad tears his hair with despair.

Dad is terribly proud of our garden
so he fills in the holes,
And then he mows what's left of
  the lawn,
And when Rover starts digging,
Dad turns the hose full on his nose!

Angela Douglas / Liz Wood

A curious young girl whose name was Amanda,
Thought it fun to behave like a green salamander,
But when she ate slugs, and hid under rugs,
Her mum said, 'Amanda, that's naughty' and banned her!

Ken Livingstone / David English

The tallest man I ever did meet
Was nine foot six in his stockinged feet.
But the rumour was, and I think it true,
With his stockings off, he was four foot two.

Ronnie Barker / David McKee

There once were three owls in a wood
Who sang songs whenever they could.
What the words were about
You couldn't make out
But it seemed to be doing them good!

Peter Wright/Colin Hawkins

A frugal feuilletonist named Heinz
Composed limericks of only two lines.

Keith Waterhouse/Patrick Benson

A young man who was visiting Bude
Went to bathe on the beach in the nude.
When they cried, 'Dirty rat!'
He just put on his hat
And said, 'Now I'm not nearly so rude.'

Roald Dahl / Quentin Blake

There was a young man from Kent
Who lived in a small green tent.
He said with a grin,
'It's a good job I'm thin,
'cause the council don't charge me much rent.'

Mark Edmonds/Julie Lacome

There was a young bat in a cave
Who was clever and cheerful and brave.
He hung by his toes
And said,
'Nobody knows
The amount of shoe leather I save.'

Michael Aspel/Joe Wright

Fergus Ewan is my name.
When I was on the climbing frame
Mummy said that I should stop,
But I climbed right up to the top
And crawled all round it on my knees.
Dad held me by my dungarees.

But when I tried to climb back down
And Dad told me to turn around,
Then I didn't feel so steady,
Dad let go, I wasn't ready.
That is when I slipped and fell
And banged my head and knees as well.
My leg felt very, very sore,
I couldn't stand up any more.

Dad said I should move my toes.
They wouldn't move, so off we go
To hospital, and there I lay
Quite still while doctors made X-ray
Pictures of my leg and head,
Then sent me to another bed.
And that was in this big room where
They tied my legs up in the air.

Mike Maran / Sarah Pooley

MARIGOLDS

I bought a bottle of Nettle Shampoo
this morning.
When I got home I wondered
Whether I shouldn't shampoo
the marigolds
as well.

Adrian Henri / Shirley Hughes

When they all went on strike at Pan Am
a highjacker highjacked a tram.
They said, 'Man, we're not fliers!'
so he shot out their tyres
and stumbled off muttering, 'Damn!'

Rolf Harris

ODE TO A GOLDFISH

O

Wet

Pet!

Gyles Brandreth/Martin Baynton

There was a young man from Tralee
Who was stung on the leg by a wasp.
When asked if it hurt
He said, 'No, not at all,
It can do it again if it likes.'

Kenny Everett/Gill Tomblin

THE SILLY SIPPOSARK

'It's not going to rain,
    So I won't come in the Ark.
The other animals are being daft,'
    Said the silly Sipposark.

Brian Patten / Anthony Browne

LARRY'S LEGS

Larry's legs go into his trousers,
Every morning at eight.
They don't mind the dark at all,
It's washing that they hate.

At bathtime when the tub is full,
His kneecaps scowl and frown.
They don't mind the suds and soap,
They're frightened they may drown.

Leon Baxter/Raymond Briggs

It's easy to be a starter,
But are you a sticker too?
It's easy enough to begin a job,
It's harder to see it through.

Margaret Thatcher/Babette Cole

There's an awful lot of weirdos
  In our neighbourhood!
Yes, there's an awful lot of weirdos
  In our neighbourhood!

I know this physical wreck,
  Who has a bolt through his neck!
There's an awful lot of weirdos
  In our neighbourhood.

And in an upstairs room,
  An old lady rides a broom!
There's an awful lot of weirdos
  In our neighbourhood.

A man lives on the square,
  When he's in he isn't there!
There's an awful lot of weirdos
  In our neighbourhood.

And that woman down the block,
 Whose snaky hair's a shock!
There's an awful lot of weirdos
 In our neighbourhood.

And someone near the dairy,
 When the moon is out gets hairy!
There's an awful lot of weirdos
 In our neighbourhood.

There's a guy who's green and scaly,
 Has webbed feet and sells fish daily!
There's an awful lot of weirdos
 In our neighbourhood.

We've a strange old feller,
 With horns, down in the cellar!
There's an awful lot of weirdos
 In our neighbourhood.

Think I'll leave this miscellanea,
 And return to Transylvania,
'cause there's an awful lot of weirdos
 In our neighbourhood!

Colin McNaughton

There once was a teacher called Leech
Who took us all down to a beach.
It said on a sign,
'Beware of the mine'.
The last thing we heard was his screech.

Michelle Gillen / Rodney Peppé

There was a young woman from Horton,
Who had a long ear and a short un,
To make up for this loss
She ate candyfloss,
That she bought from Mason and Fortnum.

Simon Groom / David Mostyn

RHYMIN' WYMAN

There once was a guy named Bill Wyman
   Who was not very hot with his rhymin'
He met a man named Brian Jones
   Who formed a band called the Stones
With a now-famous singer called Jagger

They played music all over the land
   And became the best rock 'n' roll band
Over sixty gold discs
   Topped the best-selling lists
For twenty-two years and still going

They were the first with long hair
   No stage clothes, at that time, was rare
But rebels they were then
   Five angry young men
And the press had the time of their lives

They came through it with a smile
   They've seen the world change to their style
Everyone knows them
   Wherever they go
And I can't rhyme this last line either!!

Bill Wyman / Leon Baxter

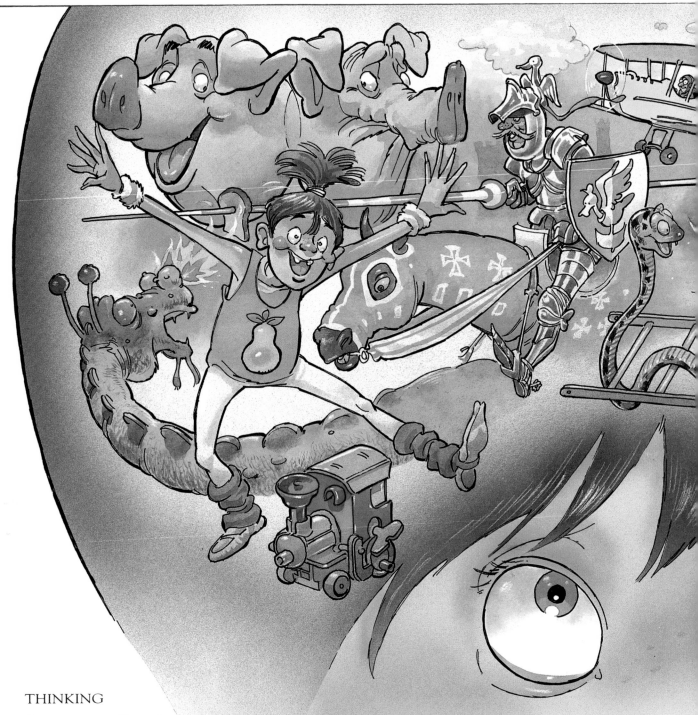

THINKING

Susie was a silly girl
Her head was always in a whirl
Just crammed with bits of this and that –
Like was she thin – or was she fat?
Would it rain, or would it snow?
Or, did her slip hang down below?
Did her hair look best on top?
Or, should she walk, or should she hop?

And – what to wear would drive her mad,
(And should she join the latest fad?)
Could she sing, or should she dance?
It seemed her thoughts were in a trance.

I wish you'd learn to *use* your head . . .
For more important things instead
Like – what do *other* people do,
Not only what is 'best for you'.
If you could look around and see
A bit beyond just you and me
You'd start to learn, and use your brain,
You wouldn't always just complain.

So – Susie tried and, do you know,
Her silly brain began to grow.
Instead of boring bits of stuff
Inside her head collecting fluff
She learnt to think, for her quite rare,
She thought of life – not of her hair.
She looked at other people's views,
She even learnt to read the news.

Her head's now filled with thoughts of sharing
Just *thinking* made her much more caring.

Nanette Newman / Alastair Graham

ON THE BREAKFAST BEAT

It drives me quite berserk
To rise each day at three,
Appalling hours to work
But, ah! that cup of tea.

They said I'd never last
The alarm with chilling call.
My friends, they stop aghast
That I make it here at all.

My face at three's a fright,
A map of lines and grief
In truth, an awful sight
But tea bears sweet relief.

A night on town's taboo.
Sure, you mustn't show it.
Alas, one fact's too true
I'll never make a poet!

Nick Owen/David Scott

LULLABY

My granny used to sing to me.
    Her voice was very deep.
She sang, 'Hush-a-bye, my baby'
    Until she fell asleep.
Then I jumped out of my cradle.
    I danced about the floor.
I shouted, 'Listen to my granny's song...

   SNORE! SNORE! SNORE!'

David Lloyd/Charlotte Voake

If you look in the eyes of a dog, you will find
They appear sentimental and gentle and kind
And they're trusting and warm. But you cannot say that
If you look in the eyes of the usual cat,
Which are selfish and cold. If you look in the eyes
Of a horse, you might (wrongly) suppose they were wise,
And there isn't much sense to be seen, I will vow,
If you look in the eyes of the average cow
Which are sleepy and sloppy and silly and sad.
If you look in the eyes of a sheep, they are mad.

But the very next time that you meet with a pig,
Have a look in its eyes. They are not very big,
Not especially lovely or notably fine,
But then look at them closely and see how they shine.
For they shine (like your own do, we hope) with a glow
Of the highest intelligence. Look and you'll know
That there isn't a doubt that a pig, by the light
In its eyes, is, compared to all other beasts, bright.
If you look in the eyes of a pig, there's no doubt
Someone very like you is in there looking out.

Dick King-Smith / Priscilla Lamont

THE KEY TO SUCCESS!

In any game, job or hobby
There's only one place to stop,
Not at the bottom or the middle
But always aim for the top!

Michael Sundin / David Bennett

There was a young man from Zaire
Whose hobby was bottling beer,
But the fumes from the brew
Turned his grandmother blue
And his grandfather green for a year.

Paul Eddington / Clive Scruton

My dogs are corgis called Kate and Cora,
they're quite fond of fauna and love most flora.
But they never thought
when they were bought
that after two years
they'd share the house
with a beautiful ginger tom cat
called Zebedee.

Penelope Keith/Louise Voce

My name is Steven
And I'm uneven.

Tony Benstead/Roger Hargreaves

Some people smell of fish and chips,
Some people smell of roses,
But none of us would smell at all
If none of us had noses.

Sally Magnusson/Norman Stone

There once was a woman
who lived by a lake,
but the house that she built
was proved a mistake.
When it slid down the hill
as spring rains sent it floating,
she announced from the porch,
'What a nice day for boating!'

Gary Bond / E. J. Taylor

MY MOTHER'S FLIT GUN

My mother had a Flit gun,
It was not devoid of charm,
A bit of Flit
Shot out of it,
The rest shot up her arm.

Pam Ayres / Victor Ambrus

THE FLYING MOUSE

Above the houses
Late at night
A mouse can fly
Until it's light.

Michelle Cartlidge

FOX

The fox
is sly
        they say
Why?

I think he's smart
He can see in the dark
He's handsome
He's quick
He can play many a trick
      on all of us

The way he can hide and cover his tracks from
the dogs who chase him,
the farmers who hate him,
makes me want him
     to win.

Alan Bates / Kenneth Lilly

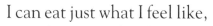

I HAVE NEVER BEEN SO HAPPY

I have never been so happy
    Since my dear old Mom and Pappy
Packed the car and left real snappy,
Said they'd had enough.

I can eat just what I feel like,
    Make up any kind of meal, like
Mars bars, chips and jellied eels, like
Mommy never made.

To nursery school I gave up going,
    They teach you nothing that's worth knowing,
And anyway there's movies showing
In the afternoons.

And bedtime, well, it's up to me now,
    Midnight, two or half past three now.
Sometimes I'll just watch TV now
All night long.

So if you're listening, Mom and Pappy,
    As you can see I'm really happy,
But could you come and change my nappy,
Mommy, Pappy, please!

Colin McNaughton / Janet Ahlberg

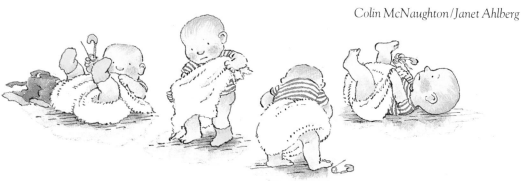

A bandsman from Barnsley called Burlington Sloane
played cornet, tenor horn, E-flat bass and trombone.
Though excessively proud,
Which we should not condone,
He did win one band contest all on his own.

Bernard Cope / Reg Cartwright

There was a young fellow named Max
Who filled all his pockets with tacks.
He thought he was clever,
Although he could never
Sit down in a chair and relax.

Sara Collis / Alfreda Benge

THE BEAR FACTS

I knew a bear
Who ate an eclair.
He reached out a paw
And ate one more.
He said: 'I do declare,
I'll give up honey
And spend my money
On things less runny.
I love eclairs,
So there.'

Tony Bradman / Jez Alborough

PLAY MAS

Play mas
Play mas
It's carnival time
So come and play mas.

Jump up
Jump up
Dance with the band
It's carnival time
So come and play mas.

Beat the drum
The steel drum
It's carnival time
So come and play mas.

Play mas
Play mas
It's carnival time
So come and play mas.

Floella Benjamin / Martin Handford

There was a young Scotsman in Rotherham,
Who had piles, which, he said, didn't botherham.
When asked to cast light
On his terrible plight,
He said, 'Och, it's nae bother at awtherham!'

Billy Connolly / Helen Oxenbury

I once knew a creature called Nelly
Who started to gobble the telly.
I begged her to cease
But she'd eaten each piece
Now there's Playschool each day in her belly.

Jane Asher/Gerald Scarfe

Maria is a little girl,
A girl of nine or ten,
She doesn't live inside a house
But in a lion's den!

Maria is a little girl,
With very curly hair,
She isn't like a timid mouse,
She's much more like a bear!

Maria is a little girl,
She seems to be quite small,
But even so she scored a goal
In Division One football!

She wears a little pinafore
Which reaches to her knee,
I really think you'd know her
If Maria you did see!

Deborah Henningham / Juan Wijngaard

UNDER THE GREENWOOD TREE...

There was one of Robin's merry men
By the name of Good Sir Ray
Who was keen to impress
By the state of his dress
So he went to C & A.

But before he set out up spake
Robin Hood,
'The choice of thy togs shall be green.
Then in leafy bower
'Twixt bud and flower
Thou art sure to remain unseen.'

'Emerald will be my own feathered cap,
In emerald I shall be swanky,
Emerald, too,
My buckle and shoe,
Why even my socks and hanky.'

But lo! He chose him garments of red!
And gave the lady tuppence.
Sir Ray, we find,
Was colour-blind
Which hath led to his comeuppance.

Mick Inkpen

A WISH COME TRUE

When I was at my mother's knee
She asked me what I'd like to be,
But all I said was 'goo ga ga'
(That's baby talk for MEGASTAR).
Now I'm beauteous, rich and wise
I look at life with older eyes
And though I am a famous Dame
Underneath I'm just the same.
Much more compassionate
          than I look –
That's why I'm writing in this book!
Each night I ask the Lord's advice:
'Please, Possum, *why am I so nice?*'

Your parents will go mad with glee
If you grow up as nice as me.

Dame Edna Everage / Ralph Steadman

I woke up one night
To an awfully loud roar
Which stopped so abruptly
I couldn't be sure
If a lion had prowled in
Then fled through the door!

Do *you* snore???

Ben Thomas / Inga Moore

Nothing is impossible!
Have you ever tried standing
a worm on end?

David Bellamy / Jan Ormerod

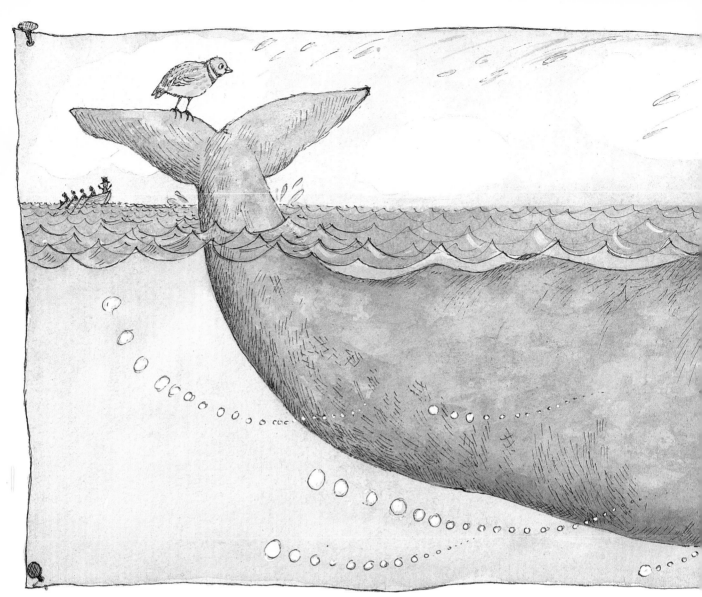

How can I fail
to tell you the tale
of the small male quail
accustomed to sail
on the rubbery tail
of a friendly old whale?

Once they wound up in jail
for putting a nail
in a bun that was stale
and feeding a snail.

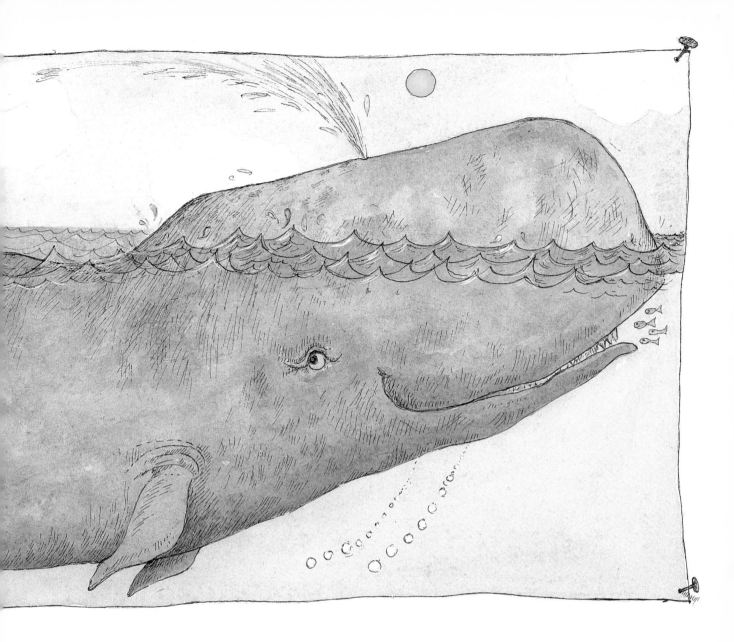

It affected her trail –
made her whimper and
wail,
and turned her quite pale.

She took to the veil…
A nun now, that snail.

Maria Aitken / Helen Craig

HELEN CRAIG

Down along the hedgerow, underneath the trees,
Gathering the blackberries, and honey from the bees,
Nuts by the basketful, plenty for the store,
And plenty for the little mouse who lives next door.

Jill Barklem

THE MIRROR

I am me,
Me I am.
Am I me?
I think I am.

Lee Radley / Graham Percy

The unicorn is a mythical beast –
Here's one that doesn't mind in the least.
Strings show him to be a bit of a phoney,
But nevertheless, well-balanced pony.

Tony Hart

When Granny went down to visit the sea,
She fell for an ice-cream seller
With black wavy hair and matching moustache,
A really handsome fella.
As a watery moon rose over the sea,
He asked, 'Please tell me, Gran,
Is it me that you love, or just my ice-cream?'
'To be honest,' she said, 'it's your van!'

Jasper Carrott/Nick Price

SORRY

You know you said I could do some cooking
And you know you said you wouldn't be looking
'cos I wanted to give you a nice surprise
And make a few cakes, make a few pies.
But you said OK. You did say yes
Well I'm really sorry, but there's a bit of a mess.
I mean to say, in about an hour
You can use quite a lot of flour
So don't get angry when you come in the door
But most of the flour is on the floor.
The rolling pin seems to be covered in dirt
And milk has soaked right through my shirt
A bit of butter has stuck to the chair
Though most of it seems to be in my hair
Yes, I can guess just what you think.
And the raisins. I forgot. They're in the sink.
So I'm really sorry, but I didn't finish the cakes.
Like you say . . . we all make mistakes.

Michael Rosen/Nick Butterworth

Outside the front door of The Bear
A clog dancer leapt in the air
But a low-flying clog
Hit the landlady's dog
So he won't be invited back there!

Pam Ayres/Nick Butterworth

MOONLIGHT DANCING

We're moonlight dancing
All alone in our rooms
We brave the storm
We're all special
We're all somebody's hero.

Toyah Willcox/Jill Murphy

MONEY IS IMPORTANT

There was an old writer of rhymes
who went through some very hard times.
He hadn't the sense
to tell pounds from pence
and he couldn't sort dollars from dimes!

Gavin Ewart/Louise Brierley

'I'm off to join the Navy,'
said Jack fleetingly.
'This is the front of my ship,'
the Captain said proudly.
'This is the back of my ship,'
the Captain said sternly.
'I've just fallen off the
Isle of Wight ferry,'
said Jack in-Solent-ly.
'I'm going to a funeral,'
said the Captain gravely.

David Frost/Gerrard McIvor

I'm not asleep.
I open my curtains,
The street lights are out,
But the stars are on!
That's when I like to talk to you,
My invisible friend.
I talk to you about the day,
I talk to you about the night,
I talk to you about everything.
It's great to have
a secret friend.

Nick Butterworth/Roy Gerrard